Presented to

....

By

....

On This Date

....

QUIET WHISPERS FROM God's Heart FOR PARENTS

JOHN TRENT, Ph.D.

an you name the person who left the first set of
footprints on the moon?

That's right, Neil Armstrong.

But can you name the man who left the *second?*

Like tracks in new-fallen snow, Buz Aldrin left his footprints
in two inches of lunar dust three minutes after Armstrong.

Imagine if you'd been able to share that experience.

Blasting off, traveling half-a-million miles from earth, and
actually walking on the moon. What thoughts would have
gone through your mind?; what feelings, what memories
would remain?

Twenty years after his return, Aldrin was asked just such a
question. At a ceremony commemorating their mind-boggling
achievement, a reporter asked, *"What remains your most vivid
memory of your trip into space?"*

Can you guess his answer?

Perhaps it was the incredible eight-and-a-half minutes
spent sitting atop a guided missile that generated *1,230,000
pounds of thrust* as it jerked and finally broke him free from the
earth's gravity?

Maybe it was the memory of that beautiful blue ball out of
the window that was Mother Earth, or the dramatic re-entry,
which produced more g-force and violent shaking than at
liftoff, coupled with temperatures soaring to levels that could
melt rock on earth?

After *twenty years,* what picture would he pick from his

mental photo album? Certainly something big . . . something dramatic . . . something loud and brash.

His most vivid memory?

"When we separated from the command module and began our descent to the moon."

Out of all the pictures to choose from . . . *that one? Why?*

"It's hard to explain, but with no gravity, the separation was . . . well . . . like a baby's breath . . ."

Two decades had passed, yet something barely noticeable . . . easily missed by others . . . held the power to leave the most vivid memory in his mind. Out of all the sights and sounds and fury of a trip to the moon, it was a *whisper* that spoke the loudest to Aldrin.

Just like when God's Spirit whispers to us.

What God uses most often to reach the deepest part of our mind and memory is that quiet nudge of His Spirit. Whispers . . . not whirlwinds. Little things . . . not laser shows.

In the stories, verses, and thoughts that follow, it's my prayer that you'll sense Someone speaking to you in quiet ways.

Take this book with you in the car as you wait to pick up your son or daughter from practice. Cultivate moments when the kids are down and the house quiet (or if you have toddlers or teenagers, at least *reasonably* quiet). Slip into the words like a warm bath. Most of all, listen for those quiet whispers of Truth from the Lover of your soul.

Yours in leaning forward to hear His voice,

JOHN TRENT, PH.D.
PRESIDENT, *ENCOURAGING WORDS*
SEPTEMBER 1999

CONTENTS

am privileged to take part in a number of radio talk programs across the country. Most are done over the phone, but occasionally I get to drop in on a radio station for a live interview. That's what happened one day when I rushed into a station at the last minute and ran into an amazing young man.

The talk show host was named Danny. He had a great smile and precious spirit. It was obvious that he loved his job and genuinely cared for the callers and listeners. He also happened to be a paraplegic since birth.

After a wonderful interview, we had a few moments to talk before his next guest.

"John," he asked, "do you want to know *why* I do a radio show?"

"Absolutely," I said.

"It's because someone handed me a light . . ."

His words were left hanging without explanation.

"Okay," I said, "I'll bite . . . what kind of light?"

"The kind that lights a path towards God's best."

He shared with me a story from his life. During junior high school, while most boys and girls felt a certain degree of insecurity, he was utterly awash in self-doubts. While others worried about acne or what to wear to the school dance, he struggled with just getting in and out of classrooms that, in the 1960s, weren't designed to accommodate wheelchairs.

He felt lonely and left out. Most of all, he felt like God could never use him to do anything significant. That is, until the day his parents switched churches, and he entered Mr. Barton's Sunday school class.

Mr. Barton had taught the junior high class at that church for years—which was a good thing. It seemed no one else wanted the challenge of facing a rowdy bunch of preteens each Sunday. But Mr. Barton not only loved junior high kids, he was also a specialist at shedding light on their paths.

There is always one moment in childhood when the door opens and lets in the future.

GRAHAM GREENE

One Sunday after the bell rang, as the kids began to run out and meet their parents, Mr. Barton called Danny's name and asked him to stay behind.

"Danny, do you know why I call on you every week in class?" he asked.

"Because I'm a good reader?" Danny asked. He'd already noticed that Mr. Barton asked him to read the Scripture passage each week.

"You are a good reader . . . but it's more than that."

And then he switched on the light for Danny that changed his life. "It's because you have such a great voice, Danny," he said. "You know . . . *I wouldn't be surprised if God ended up using your voice to serve Him someday.* Ever thought about being a pastor or speaker or Christian DJ?"

Fifteen words, spoken in under seven seconds, changed the course of Danny's life. They became a shining path toward a special future—and they're the reason he's a radio talk-show

9

host today.

In Jeremiah 29:11, God gives us a wonderful promise we can pass down to our children. *"For I know the plans that I have for you,' declares the Lord . . . 'plans . . . to give you a future and a hope'"* (NASB).

Mom and Dad, look for ways to light up your child's future.

Help them see by your words and genuine praise that their unique gifts or talents are attributes God can use for His glory.

Just like Mr. Barton did for Danny.

Ask people to draw up a list of positive parenting attributes, and you'll likely get a list of words like *loving, sensitive, caring, nurturing*—all good words and traits.

But in this day and age, there's another word that is crucial: *Courage.*

Recently, a Christian mother was shocked to find a sexually explicit book on her ten-year-old's "encouraged reading" list. She took her complaint to the teacher and was treated with scorn. The principal said, *"You're the only one who's complained."* She received a lecture on the evils of "censorship" and "First Amendment" rights, not a listening ear. Her daughter was later ridiculed by several children for having such "restrictive" views and parents.

Taking a stand to protect your child's purity or to defend biblical values takes courage—the courage to step out and do what's right.

But then again . . . it has *always* taken courage to do what's right.

Go back to December 14, 1862.

On that day, one man stepped out . . . and an entire battle stopped.

With the Civil War raging, Union soldiers from Colonel Joshua L. Chamberlain's Second Maine regiment charged across a plowed cornfield a dozen times, trying to take a hill called Marye's Heights in Fredericksburg, Virginia. Valor alone wasn't enough to take the hill.

At the end of the field was a stone wall heavily defended by Confederate troops. They poured murderous rifle and canister shot into the advancing Union troops and hundreds fell dead or wounded. In twelve attempts, not one Union solider made it to the stone wall.

Chamberlain was to recount, "My ears were filled with the cries and groans of the wounded. The ghastly faces of the dead almost made a wall around me."

With each wave, the dead and wounded piled up. They lay suffering in the December cold, bleeding to death slowly on the open plain, wracked by pain and thirst brought upon them by their wounds.

But then one man moved.

Sergeant Richard Rowland Kirkland of the Second South Carolina Confederate States Army felt he "had to do something in the name of Christ."

He loaded himself with over a dozen borrowed canteens, then leapt over the wall and walked to the nearest Union sufferer. He knelt and gave him water and made him more comfortable . . .then he moved on to the next man . . . and the next.

For *the next hour and a half,* not one shot was fired from either side.

A battle was stopped because one man had the power to step out.

Lord, as we face the spiritual and emotional battles that will come as Christian parents, give us courage. Help us to step out and do what's right . . . even if it means stepping into a cultural or moral battlefield. Amen.

Be strong and of good courage; do not be afraid, nor be dismayed, for the Lord your God is with you wherever you go.

JOSHUA 1:9

SOME PEOPLE JUST HAVE TO SEE IT TO BELIEVE IT

haron was a doubter.

Not that she meant to be.

But it had been hammered into her emotional makeup. Her father had left when she was six—the same man who had a pattern of calling and saying to her, "I'm coming over to see you!" and then, after Karen spent hours expectantly looking out of the window, wouldn't show up. Karen would finally go to her room and cry over another broken promise.

And it wasn't just her father.

Within six months of her parents' divorce, her mother married a man who said from day one, "You're my wife first . . . her mother second."

She had a distant father and then lost what little relationship she had with her mother.

Broken dreams . . . broken promises . . . broken hearts.

That's the stuff doubt is made of. And it's no wonder that doubt carried forward into her own marriage. Try as she might, she felt as secure with her husband as an eighty-five year old does when walking on black ice.

Not that he gave her reason.

He was an outstanding Christian man from a warm, loving home. He had Job's patience in staying consistent through their four-year courtship (even through the three times she broke their engagement!). In eight years of marriage, he'd never given her reason to doubt his love.

But she just couldn't see it . . . until the day the insurance nurse came.

Alan was getting a physical for a new insurance policy,

which required a nurse to take his blood and give him an EKG. The male nurse showed up first thing in the morning, and when the EKG was over, Alan walked back to their bedroom to shower and dress for work.

All I have seen teaches me to trust the creator for all I have not seen.

RALPH WALDO EMERSON

That's when it happened.

As the nurse was putting away the EKG machine and gathering his things, he said to Sharon, "You're a lucky woman. Your husband really loves you."

"Why . . . thank you," she said, slightly embarrassed, ready for him to finish and leave.

"I mean it," he said, not moving from the room, "I can prove it to you."

"You can do what?" Sharon asked.

"I can prove to you that your husband loves you . . . just look at this." And then he laid out the strip of paper from the EKG machine.

Pointing to the lines the machine had made, he said, "This is where your husband's heartbeat and blood pressure were during the first half of the test," he said, pointing to a long stretch of similar lines, all at relatively the same height.

"And this is when you walked into the room . . . His heartbeat and blood pressure jumped when he saw you."

Tears of joy flooded Sharon's eyes.

17

Finally . . . she *"got the picture"* that her husband really, truly loved her—one she couldn't deny.

Mom . . . Dad . . . it's not just a wife from a difficult background who needs to see it to believe it. There's a bit of doubting Thomas in us all . . . even in our kids.

Today, give them "a picture" of your love by kneeling by their bed and praying with and for them. Send them to school with a note that says, "Out of all the kids your age in the world . . . we'd pick you." Welcome them home with bright eyes and an unexpected treat.

They'll "get the picture" without your having to take an EKG.

I n the wonderful book by Ken Gire entitled *Windows of the Soul,* there's the story of a happy-go-lucky young girl who lived at the edge of a forest. She loved to hunt flowers and explore the green pastures and woodlands. But one day, as the shadows grew long, she lost her way.

When she didn't return for supper, her parents began to search for her. They repeatedly called her name, then asked the neighbors to help them hunt for their loved one. During that time, their daughter was scared and lost, wandering deeper and deeper into the forest. Exhausted, she crawled upon a large rock, laid her tear-stained head down on that hard pillow, and fell asleep.

In the first light of day, after hunting all night, the father finally spotted his young daughter. There she was, asleep on a rock in the middle of a clearing. He ran as fast as he could, calling out her name.

The noise awakened the girl. She sat up suddenly, her eyes beaming.

As her face exploded into a smile, she reached for her father and said, "Daddy! . . . *I found you!*"

Isn't that just like a child?

They can feel so vulnerable, so lonely, so lost. Then, when they're rescued by someone who has *purposely sought them out,* they say, "I found you, Mommy . . . I found you, Daddy."

This whispers a question to parents.

Dad, does your son or daughter wake up after a tough day at school and "find" a note that you're praying for them? Mom, after they've lost a best friend or have been hassled for being the only outspoken Christian in their school, do they "find" you hugging away the hurt?

If they do, you're doing a good job of acting like your Heavenly Father.

Hundreds of years ago, God's people labored in bondage far from their home. Every day, they woke up alone and forsaken, surrounded by a hostile nation. But listen to the promise God personally gave them:

Talk cheerily to the young and anxious inquirer, lovingly try to remove stumbling blocks out of his way.

CHARLES SPURGEON

"For thus says the Lord God: 'Indeed I Myself will search for My sheep and seek them out'" (Ezek. 34:11).

Almighty God Himself sought out His loved ones in the midst of hurt and heartache.

He came to *them.*

Mom . . . Dad . . . do you know your child's fears and heartaches?

Does she "find" you praying for her?

Do you search out ways to bless and encourage him?

Jesus says, *"I will not leave you orphans; I will come to you"* (John 14:18).

21

GAINING HEIGHT BY LOWERING THE BAR

ewind your memory banks to 1992.

In anticipation of the summer Olympic Games, Reebok invested over *fifteen million dollars* in ads asking whether the world's greatest decathlete was Dan O'Brien or Dave Johnson. Would it be "Dan or Dave" at the finish? Each was considered a "slam dunk" to make the Olympic team, compete in Barcelona, and go for the gold.

At the U.S. Olympic trials, the two were indeed neck-and-neck in points, until the pole vault event. That competition started at 14' 5¼". O'Brien had jumped this height, and higher, literally hundreds of times. He considered this event one of his best. So he decided to pass on the opening height. He didn't take off his warm-ups until his opening jump came at 15' 9".

On his first attempt, he went *under* the bar. *No problem.* On his second attempt, he knocked the bar off coming *down.* Now everyone in the stands (especially the Reebok executives) began to think . . . *maybe there's a problem.* On his third and final attempt, he ran down the runway, plated his pole, . . . and went *under* the bar again.

If O'Brien had just cleared the opening height, he would have earned enough points to make the Olympic team and have had a chance at the gold. But he didn't. He spent the 1992 Olympics in the broadcasting booth rather than on the field.

Mom . . . Dad . . . can you hear God whispering in that story about your role as a parent?

When Israel took the Promised Land, they did it one step, one city at a time. Being a godly parent is all about making the opening height . . . not setting the bar at 15' 9". Let me explain.

Frequently, I meet people who think their role as a parent

is to "Go for the gold!"

They say, "None of this ten minutes of focused attention before bedtime . . . I'm going to spend an hour minimum playing with my kids twice a day." "Forget that book of daily devotionals for kids—I'm going to develop my own quiet-time materials for each child!" These are the same parents who raise the bar by "committing" to *never* losing their temper again or to *always* putting the paper down when the kids want to talk or play.

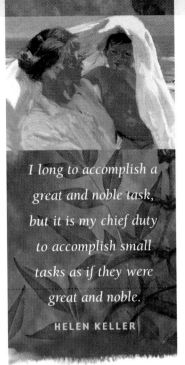

I long to accomplish a great and noble task, but it is my chief duty to accomplish small tasks as if they were great and noble.

HELEN KELLER

What happens when these parents knock the bar off once or twice? They often throw up their hands and give up altogether.

Let me ask you a difficult question: Is God asking you to lower the bar as a parent?

Wouldn't it be better if you took off your sweats early and hit the opening height first—like giving Suzie one hug each day, telling Steven you love him before bed, following through on family rules, or going to church as a family this Sunday?

Low-bar stuff. The kind of things the Lord calls "faithfulness." Being there. Keeping your promises. Doing what you say.

Where's the bar set in your home?

"May the Lord repay every man for his righteousness and his faithfulness" (1 Sam. 26:23).

ADDITION OR SUBTRACTION?

Did you know that every day, you're choosing to add or subtract?

I'm not talking about doing flash cards with the kids or balancing the checkbook at home.

I'm referring to the choice we make each day, as parents and people who love Jesus, to add or subtract. Put in biblical terms, *to bless or to curse*.

Do you know what the biblical meaning of the word *bless* is?

When we sing, "Bless the Lord, Oh my soul!" or read that the Lord is worthy to be "blessed," it literally means He is "heavy, weighty," worthy to be "bowed before." The meaning comes from gold that is weighed out on scales. The more weight added, the more valuable. So when we bless the Lord

or our children, we're adding "weight" to their words or person.

Do you know what the word *curse* means in the Scriptures? It's used to describe a stream that has dried up to a muddy trickle because water has been "subtracted" from it.

From the first "curse" that fell upon Adam and Eve for their sin, you can see the idea of "subtraction" linked to it. Their choice to disobey took away Eden and subtracted life from them as well.

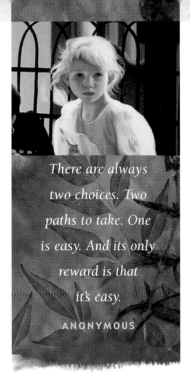

There are always two choices. Two paths to take. One is easy. And its only reward is that it's easy.

ANONYMOUS

What does this have to do with parenting?

Every day, we've got a choice set before us.

Literally.

Whether we're a parent or pastor.

Teenager or grandparent.

Accountant or welder.

Husband or wife.

The Bible puts it this way, *"I have set before you life and death, blessing and cursing; therefore, choose life"* (Deut. 30:19).

It's up to you.

Are you "adding" positive words, prayers, and extra "weight" to your loved ones? Or subtracting?

25

I ran into an interesting historical fact the other day. It had to do with the incredible lengths one culture went to in order to keep *pride* from ruining their country.

It seems that in 510 B.C., the Athenians fought a war to overthrow one of their own. His name was Hippias, and he was once the "golden boy" of Athens. Yet as his popularity rose, so too did his ambition. And with ambition came a grab for power, and hundreds of lives were lost putting down his insurrection.

Wanting to learn from the coup attempt, their parliament convened and talked through what happened.

Their conclusion: Pride had nearly cost them their kingdom. Their solution: Strict rules to avoid another display of tyranny.

From that day forward, once a year there would be a special election by the Athenians. Not aimed at *electing* someone, but at *exiling* him! Each Athenian was required to write down the name of a politician he felt was growing too ambitious, too strong, too greedy or powerful for the good of the state.

If one man received a majority of the total votes, he was forced to leave Athens for ten years. It was not a disgraceful exile: His property was not confiscated, and his family was not mistreated. When the decade was up, he was welcomed back. But he understood that he had been sent away to avoid the temptation of trying to upset the democracy (Isaac Asimov's *Book of Facts*).

Before you dismiss these ancient Athenians' actions as "ancient history" (which, of course, it is!), think of what they tried to do in setting up this vote—namely, reward team builders, not win-at-all-costs types. They cut down pride instead of cultivating it.

Mom . . . Dad . . . can you see any application to your home?

You certainly can in God's Word.

A "measly" fifty-five times in God's Word, the word *pride* is mentioned.

From the fall of Satan . . . to the arrogance of Pharaoh . . . to the ego of Herod . . . to the pride the very disciples felt when they argued over who was the greatest.

Nothing sets a person so much out of the devil's reach as humility.

JONATHAN EDWARDS

But you never see *pride* in reference to our Lord Jesus.

I'm all for encouraging kids to do their best. To be all they can be.

To go for the gold and their dreams.

But sinful pride means more than that. It means going for the jugular, walking over weaker kids, choosing selfishness over serving.

The answer to unhealthy pride in a child isn't found in shaming them. It's in teaching them to be like Jesus . . . the servant of all. Someone who "made Himself of no reputation, taking the form of a bondservant, and . . . became obedient to the point of death, even the death of the cross" (Phil. 2:7-8).

In our power-hungry, winning-is-everything culture, take a vote in your home.

Make a decision to exile unhealthy pride, and watch your family become more like Christ.

27

ust look at the headlines.

Sports stars . . . politicians . . . super models . . . world leaders . . . even major criminals get front page attention.

But don't count on coverage if you're a parent.

See any headlines lately declaring, "Parents of Preteen with Major Attitude Problem Given Medal for Patience"? Or, "Dedicated Dad Earns Nobel Prize for Coaching Yet Another of His Kid's Sports Teams"?

Not likely in our lifetime. In fact, when it comes to recognition for your job as a parent, you may go to bed feeling insignificant in the world's eyes.

But headlines don't tell the whole story. No one knew this better than Third Officer Charles Victor Groves one bitter and cold Sunday night.

Officer Groves was plodding through the Atlantic Ocean on the 6,000-ton cargo ship, the *Californian*, bound from London to Boston.

At 11:10 p.m., Groves noticed the lights of another ship racing up on his starboard side. The newcomer, its decks ablaze with lights, rapidly overtook the *Californian*. It was a *66,000-ton* ship, with triple screws that could make nearly thirty knots compared to his ship's sluggish ten. Three thousand people had chosen this beautiful liner for their transatlantic trip, including many who captured headlines in their day.

Third Officer Groves said, "When I went to bed that night, I remember thinking how insignificant my ship was compared to the display I'd just seen."

Little did he know that just thirty minutes later, all of the pomp and pageantry racing past him would become one of the world's greatest tragedies. At 11:40 p.m., on April 14, 1912, the *Titanic* would veer sharply to port, rake an iceberg at starboard, and send fifteen hundred men, women, and children to their deaths.

> *I found Him in the shining of the stars, I marked Him in the flowering of His fields.*
>
> **ALFRED LORD TENNYSON**

In the Old Testament, David may have gone to sleep one night feeling like Third Officer Groves. Even with the arrival of a special guest, David was left to watch over his sheep instead of changing into party dress.

Yet without complaint, David remained faithfully at his post, taking care of little lambs who needed a shepherd, even as Jesse paraded his sons before the prophet Samuel.

"And Samuel said to Jesse, 'Are all the young men here?' Then he said, 'There remains yet the youngest, and there he is, keeping the sheep.' And Samuel said to Jesse, 'Send and bring him. For we will not sit down till he comes here'" (1 Sam. 16:11).

When the group finally did sit down, it was to honor the one left standing: King David, a nobody that somebody noticed.

29

Much of the time, parenting has all the excitement of being the third officer on a cargo ship . . . and all the responsibility of being a shepherd whose devotion to his sheep keeps him out of the society pages. But Almighty God sees and knows and rewards your faithfulness.

This morning when you read the headlines, or this evening when you watch the late news, realize that many "stars" and celebrities in the fast lane are coursing straight into personal or spiritual tragedy—but you stay at your post. Headlines or not, you're a *somebody* to Someone who knows, loves, and sees your commitment to your family.

FRAMING POSITIVE PICTURES OF FAITH

Did you know that an important way to strengthen your children's faith is by teaching them to frame pictures? In this quiet whisper and the next, I urge you to become proficient in your matting and hammering skills. Not for framing paintings or color prints, but for framing pictures you create with your words, eyes, and ears. These are the "frames" you put around the mental and emotional pictures your children bring home each day . . . pictures of a frowning face stamped on a school paper or a gold star stuck to an assignment. Or even cruel pictures handed them on the playground, or long-sought-after encouragement from a coach.

Good or bad, these will remain with them for years.

For many children, the pictures they receive in the crucial "growing up" years determine the type of person they will become. That's why it's so important to "frame" the positive pictures—especially those pictures of faith— and help them "reframe" negative ones.

Let's look first at framing positive pictures—a skill our Lord perfected in His dealings with His loved ones.

One day, Jesus asked the disciples, "Who do you say I am?" Peter alone stepped forward.

"You are the Christ, the Son of the Living God."

Jesus didn't shrug off this bold pronouncement; instead, he put a "frame" around it, praising Peter by saying, "Blessed are you, Simon Bar-Jonah, for flesh and blood has not revealed this to you, but My Father who is in heaven" (Matt. 16:17).

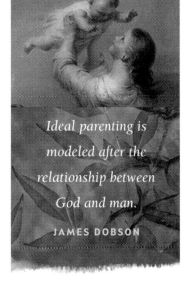

Ideal parenting is modeled after the relationship between God and man.

JAMES DOBSON

Jesus provided a frame around that positive confession of faith, creating a picture that Peter could hang on the walls of his heart and draw strength from.

How can you frame positive declarations of faith or love made by your child? Follow the example of two parents in our neighborhood.

Our friends have a very active, "all-sports, all-the-time" son. Most dinner conversations revolve around his favorite sports team's standings or struggles. But one night, their eight year old made an announcement that dropped jaws, stopped forks in midair, and warmed hearts.

"I'm giving up candy for an entire week," he announced with great conviction.

At first, his mom and dad thought they were getting ready to hear an admission of guilt for some offense. Losing candy for a week must be his own "punishment" for doing wrong.

It was a confession all right . . . but one of faith in Christ.

"We talked about the cross today in Sunday school," he said. "And I decided that if Jesus gave up that much for me, then I'm going to give up candy for a week to say I love Him."

These parents did not attend church and did not come from a tradition where Lent is observed. But their son's words came right from his heart, in response to looking at the cross and at how much Jesus gave to buy us back from sin.

Dad . . . Mom . . . when you see or hear your son share with a friend instead of being selfish, turn that act of sharing into a "picture" worth saving. When your daughter asks to pray for a friend who is sick or hurting at the dinner table, point out her sensitivity. When you see them take even small steps forward in faith or love, let your words put a frame around that event.

Highlight what they did right.

Remember it at a family gathering.

Take the time to write your child a note, telling him you're proud of the choice he made or the caring act he did. Our friends did these things to frame their son's confession of faith spoken at the dinner table.

I promise . . . praising your children for taking their faith seriously won't give them a swelled head. It can give them a framed example of faith to hang in a special place in their lives . . . and to look back on for years to come.

35

REFRAMING NEGATIVE PICTURES

raming current pictures of faith can do much to help children take their faith seriously. But helping them *"reframe"* negative pictures is just as important. To understand this, let's fast-forward to another "picture" in the apostle Peter's life . . . one I'm sure he wanted to forget.

It was a cold, terrible night.

Jesus had been arrested. He was then falsely accused, went through the mockery of a trial, and was finally condemned to death. The Scriptures tell us of another event that night that added insult to Christ's coming injury.

Peter was warming himself beside a "a charcoal fire" when a servant-girl spotted him. "You are not also one of this man's disciples, are you?" she asked (John 18:17-18, NASB). Immediately, Peter denied knowing Christ.

Noting his distinct accent, however, a second servant-girl supported the charge. Again Peter denied it, this time with an oath (Matt. 26:71-72). Finally, a third time, "he began to *curse and swear,"* saying he didn't know Jesus when questioned (v. 74).

Then the cock crowded three times, and Scripture tells us that Jesus turned and looked right into Peter's eyes. Peter broke into tears of shame and would carry that pain-wrapped memory each day.

What a picture of betrayal, failure, and shame. But our Lord made sure his failure would end up *increasing* his faith . . . not adding to his shame. *How?*

Jesus "reframed" the event for Peter in a wonderfully loving way.

In the days following the crucifixion and resurrection,

Peter was still distraught over denying Christ. Like many facing shameful memories, Peter chose *activity* over just sitting and thinking.

"I am going fishing," he said to the disciples (John 21:3), who decided to join him.

They fished all night but caught nothing—that is, until a stranger called to them from the shore.

"Children, you do not have any fish, do you?" he asked them (v. 5).

We are not saviors, but we can help others toward faith. This means not only loving them while they're still in the mire, but loving them out of it.

ELISABETH ELLIOT

When they answered no, He called to them to let down their nets. In the record catch that followed, these fishermen's eyes were opened to see who was on the beach.

"*It is the Lord,*" they said.

Peter threw himself in the water and swam to shore. There, Jesus had a fish supper waiting . . . and a "charcoal fire" (v. 9).

Only two times in all of the New Testament do you find the word *charcoal*. Once when Peter sat over a "charcoal fire" and denied Christ. The second here on the beach . . . a fire that Jesus made.

Can you see what Jesus is doing?

He's taking Peter back to that night . . . that failure . . .

37

that negative picture of shame he still carried inside him. And in doing so, Jesus doesn't use denial, or false guilt, or positive self-help talk to make Peter feel better. Instead, He reframes the event in light of who Peter really was.

Three times, Peter had denied Christ.

Now, three times, Jesus asks Peter, Do you love me? Three times, Peter has the chance to reaffirm his love for Christ—once for each denial.

Dad . . . Mom . . . all kids make mistakes. They fail a test. They go through a friendship falling apart. Or, in some cases, like Peter, they fail a test of character. They lie, or steal, or cheat, or hurt someone. We need to discipline them (for that is a key aspect of loving them). But after the "time out," loss of privilege, or other appropriate consequence, we need to help them face what they did. Help them sit over a "charcoal fire" and learn from the event—not ignore it or pretend it never happened.

"Feed my sheep" were Christ's last words to Peter.

In modern-day words, Jesus said, "Get back to being my shepherd instead of slamming yourself. Learn from the failure. Be honest about it, but get back to being who I called you to be."

Mom . . . Dad . . . do you need to sit your children down around a "charcoal fire" to help them move on from a difficult experience?

Do you need to sit around a charcoal fire yourself?

I know what some parents may be thinking as they read this book. *Words . . . words . . . words . . .*

It always seems that the "good stories" are of really great parents who come up with just the right words at just the right time.

"But I'm just not creative!" you might say.

No problem.

Take a moment to read through the list of "words" that follow.

You don't have to be creative, or clever, or profound.

Just look for opportunities to put any one of these words or phrases into practice. When your son or daughter brings home an A paper from school or hits a double . . . Or better yet, when they get a C when they really, really tried, or when they strike out in the ninth . . . pick a word or phase to say to them.

Better yet, pick a *goal.*

Make a photocopy of this list. (*Just this one page* so the publisher doesn't become concerned!) Then take two months—*sixty days*—and look for a way to pour each one of these positive words into your child's little love bank.

Ready . . . set . . . get creative!

> *I'm proud of you*
> *Way to go*
> *Bingo . . . You did it*
> *Magnificent*
> *I knew you could do it*
> *What a good helper*

- *You're very special to me*
- *I trust you*
- *What a treasure*
- *Hooray for you*
- *Beautiful work*
- *You're a real trooper*
- *Well done*
- *That's so creative*
- *You make my day*
- *You're a joy*
- *Give me a big hug*
- *You figured it out*
- *I love you*
- *You remembered*
- *You're the best*
- *You're such a good listener*
- *You're so responsible*
- *You sure tried hard*
- *I've got to hand it to you*
- *I couldn't be prouder of you*
- *You light up my day*
- *My buttons are popping off*
- *I'm praying for you*
- *You're wonderful*
- *I'm behind you*
- *You're so kind to your (brother/sister)*
- *You're God's special gift*
- *I'm here for you*

Our words can promote growth by wrapping others in a cocoon of love and hope.

**GARY SMALLEY
AND JOHN TRENT**

The day *before* I spoke at a Promise Keepers rally in Oakland, California, I got to live out a childhood fantasy. (Okay—make that a *grown-up* fantasy!)

As the tarps went down and the thousands of chairs went up on the baseball field where the major league Oakland Athletics play, a good friend and I took turns standing at home plate.

We'd sneer at the imaginary pitcher on the mound ninety feet away . . . wait . . . then swing and "crack!"—hitting an invisible, ninety-mile-an-hour fastball out of the park. What fun it was "running the bases" of a major-league stadium for a home run!

We *played* at hitting it out of the park. But the next day, someone *did* hit a five hundred foot shot over the green wall in front of fifty thousand men. It wasn't a baseball player. It was a young man with me named Shon Stewart.

Shon is a smart, handsome, and talented eighteen year old. God has given him a wonderful voice and desire to sing for the Lord. God has also confined him to a wheelchair because of cerebral palsy.

The title of that year's conference was Break Down the Walls. I was there to talk about being a person of "commitment." But while I shared about the challenge of commitment, Shon and his father Tom gave the audience a picture of how it is lived out every day.

As Tom stood next to his son, Shon sang the words, *"Give me a heart like my father . . . kind and forgiving . . . just like the father heart of God . . ."*

It was a bases-loaded, game-winner of a song. And *every man with every excuse for why he was too busy or too tired or too*

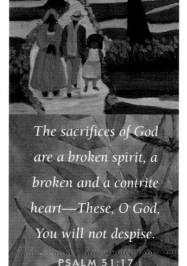

The sacrifices of God are a broken spirit, a broken and a contrite heart—These, O God, You will not despise.

PSALM 51:17

important to be a blessing to his son or daughter . . . saw his rationalizations slammed into the upper deck by Shon's song and Tom's presence.

Especially one man. Six years before, he and his wife had a baby boy.

His first child. His dream child. The son he'd always wanted.

Born just like Shon with cerebral palsy.

But unlike Tom, this man became so angry at God, his wife, and the doctors that he shut everyone out. He immediately quit going to church and made his wife feel terrible; somehow it was "her fault."

For six years, he virtually ignored his son. Then a friend (almost literally) dragged him to Promise Keepers—the first "religious" thing he'd done since his son's birth. Neither man knew Shon would be singing. Yet seeing Shon in his wheelchair brought him face-to-face with his deepest fears and inner anger. Soaking wet, Shon probably weighs about 140 pounds. But that day, God used him to "body slam" a 6' 3" man, softening his heart and sending him to his knees in repentance—and back to his wife and son who needed him so much.

Dad . . . Mom . . . while your walls are probably not as high as the walls God broke down in this man's life, consider whether the walls in your life are holding you back from being the parent He wants you to be.

43

Several years ago, I was with some fishing friends at a small restaurant in Kodiak, Alaska. We'd spent an exhausting but enjoyable fourteen-hour day catching salmon and marveling at the incredible scenery.

We were ready for a quiet meal and a chance to swap "the-one-that-got-away" stories when a small boy and his parents walked in. The boy held a chocolae ice-cream cone. Actually, *held* wasn't an accurate description. He looked like the cone had exploded all over him! Chocolate was smeared on his face, and it coated his hand and clothes.

Our table was near the door. When the chocolate-covered youngster saw my friends and I looking at him, his eyes lit up. He ran over to us, and with a giggle, he proceeded to wipe his mouth and little face on my pants!

In shock, I jumped up and cried, "What do you think you're doing?"

"Did you see what your son did?" I asked in disbelief, though his parents had watched the whole scene take place.

They just *smiled* . . . and with that reinforcement, their precious, chocolate-dipped angel drew back and threw what was left of his ice-cream cone at me—hitting me, dead-center, in the chest!

While I was considering pressing charges, the little boy triumphantly walked back to his parents and stood between them, never saying a word.

With ice cream smeared on my shirt and pants, I appealed to his parents, and they finally stepped in.

"Come on, sweetheart," the mother said after a long pause. *"We'll have to get you another ice-cream cone."*

Then they turned and walked into the next room.

To this day, I marvel at what happened that night. With those kinds of parents, I'm sure their son has grown up to lead his own Colombian drug cartel—or run for Congress!

That "chocolate-covered trauma" did teach me an important lesson. When parental leadership and discipline is

> Without the balance of love and limits, children are robbed of the wholeness God intended them to have.
>
> **GARY SMALLEY**

fragmented or nonexistent, children *and* those they come into contact with suffer. When the writer of Hebrews penned the words, "For whom the Lord loves He chastens" (12:6), it was in the context of a loving Father who steps in with correction, much like a caring mother who is strong enough to confront a wrong.

In this day and age of "high self-esteem," praise is certainly crucial for a child's well-being. Yet praise apart from correction provides as much stability in a child's life as a two-legged stool. If you skip correction, you deny a child wisdom, instruction, . . . and genuine love.

A quiet lesson can be gained from that chaotic run-in. Are we letting our children "smear" improper actions on the lives of others? Are we labeling wrong actions as "cute" ? Are we committed to godly correction?

Discipline doesn't mean blasting; it means blessing your child . . . and it just might save someone a dry-cleaning bill!

45

*No job can compete
with the responsibility
of shaping and molding
a new human being.*

JAMES C. DOBSON

PERSPECTIVE CHECK

Kari, our oldest daughter, was the "swinger" of the family when she was a toddler. Every day when I came home from work, I'd hear, *"Swing me, Daddy. Swing me, Daddy!"*

We'd go out to the porch swing while my wife Cindy was finishing dinner. It was during one of our "swinging sessions" that I got a precious lesson on the perspective of a child.

In our house, we keep all of the medicine in the highest shelves in the kitchen. Even if the kids were able to climb up on the counter when they were young, they wouldn't have been able to reach over the fan, and above the stove and the microwave oven, to the "medicine shelf."

While swinging one day, Kari explained her view of the medicine shelf.

Kari loves to sing, and she particularly liked belting out song after song as I pushed her back and forth. Her sweet little voice started into a familiar song that she hadn't sung in quite a while . . .

But now with a new twist. "Twinkle, twinkle little star. How I wonder where you are. *Up above the microwave . . .*"

From Kari's perspective, she didn't miss a beat in switching "Up above the world so high" to "Up above the microwave"—that's because from her perspective, the medicine shelf was the highest place in the world.

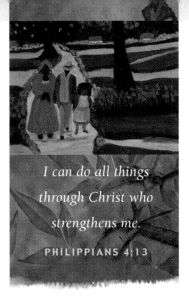

I can do all things through Christ who strengthens me.

PHILIPPIANS 4:13

Dad . . . Mom . . . have you stopped to consider the "perspective" of your child?

They see things differently when they're two feet tall . . . or when they're preteens.

Particularly when they're young, it's important to get down on their level . . . literally. To bend or kneel down at times to look at them, eye-to-eye. But at any age, it's important to become a student of how they see the world—what limits they see or what heights they're picturing for themselves.

That's one thing my own mother did exceedingly well. She took the time to try and see life from our perspective. To understand where we stood on issues and feelings. To see where the self-imposed "ceilings" were in our lives and to encourage us to lift our sights "above the microwave" to a world of opportunities beyond.

Mom . . . Dad . . . do you know the floor and ceiling of your child's worldview?

know that couples break up all the time. But as a young Christian, I never thought Alan and Marty would.

I knew affairs ruined many relationships . . . but not theirs.

I'd known that pillars of the church could walk away from a marriage . . . *but not at my church and not them!*

Out of all the Christians I'd met up to then, I'd have put them in my top 1 percent of truly committed couples.

But I was wrong.

I'd only seen one "reflection" of the mirror. I'd seen their Sunday reflection, and it was brilliant.

I didn't know there was a much darker Monday-through-Saturday version.

Alan and Marty were living in a "house of mirrors" . . . reflecting one image at church and a very different one at home or when no one was looking.

Today, some twenty years later, I understand better how such tragedies can happen. In fact, I even coined a term for this tragic phenomenon in a book I wrote, *LifeMapping.* It's called *image management,* and *it's something Christian parents need to avoid like the plague.*

Image management is the attempt to support or "manage" a public self while practicing a very different private self at home. Such inner duplicity inevitably leads to greater stress in relationships, and often, to a breakdown of values.

Just like with Alan and Marty.

Serious struggles in their marriage . . . but all smiles at church on Sunday.

Major issues from their turbulent pasts . . . yet a total

unwillingness to admit them and call for a pastor or counselor's help.

After all . . . that would have affected their "image."

The losers?

Obviously, they lost their relationship, which was brought on when one of them got tired of living two lives and left the "house of mirrors" for a series of affairs.

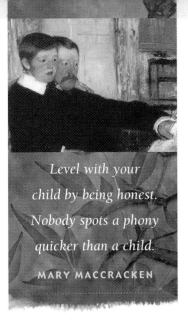

Level with your child by being honest. Nobody spots a phony quicker than a child.

MARY MACCRACKEN

But there were silent victims of their image management as well. Today, their two boys and one girl are all grown up. However, the three have something in common, besides their parents outstanding looks . . . and the divorce: Not one of them wants anything to with church or God or anything that smacks of the phony image their parents tried to pull off.

Don't misread what I'm saying. *Every parent,* to a degree (indeed, every person), has occasions when they fall or fail to live up to a calling. Yet for Alan and Marty, image management wasn't an occasional slip—it was an everyday lifestyle. They could be screaming at the children or each other one second, then be kind and sweet to a church friend on the telephone the next. That's deceit, pure and simple. And while you may be able to fool most of the people who don't live with you most of the time . . . forget faking out the kids. They're like God's little detectives.

51

Is there an antidote to image management? Is there a way out of this deadly house of mirrors?

Yes. Several.

First, be honest about your own background. If you came from a long line of image managers, don't let familiar patterns of deception pass down to your generation. Speak the truth in love. Deal with issues instead of opting for denial.

Second, don't think that image management is reserved for an elite, isolated, or faithless few. Listen to the charge our Lord brought against a group of believers that looked to all the world like sold-out saints.

"'I know your works, your labor, your patience, and that you cannot bear those who are evil,' says the Lord. 'And you have tested those who say they are apostles and are not, . . . and have not become weary'" (Rev. 2:2-3).

These believers were pros at doing things right on the *outside*. But they had a near-fatal flaw in their faith: *"Nevertheless I have this against you, that you have left your first love"* (v. 4).

Near fatal because Almighty God gives them a way out . . . an antidote to image management:

"Remember therefore from where you have fallen; repent and do the first works" (v. 5).

Remember . . . repent . . . get back to doing what's right.

Honest, challenging words for any parent serious about avoiding or escaping a destructive house of mirrors.

53

Did you know that a microwave, a balloon, or a star-filled night could become a spiritual training tool?

One mother wanted to teach her six-year-old son a lesson about anger. He had been blowing up when he got frustrated with his sister, but his mom wanted him to understand that his behavior wasn't loving.

At the dinner table one night, she and her children looked up James 1:20. There they read "the wrath of man does not produce the righteousness of God," and they talked about how anger doesn't make someone more righteous or more like Jesus. Then the mom did something to help her son "get the picture" of what that verse meant. She asked each child to fill up a microwave-safe, glass mug with water. Then, she had them put the mugs in the microwave on high power.

Within three minutes, they could see bubbles coming up from the water inside the mugs. "Now push pause," she said to her son. He did, and the bubbles in the mugs instantly stopped. They repeated this experiment several times, with her son and daughter taking turns pushing the pause button and watching the bubbles stop.

Then she asked, "Brian, when you get mad at your sister, does it feel like you have lots of bubbles inside that want to come out?"

He nodded his head, yes.

"Can you see how to be like Jesus, you need to push the 'pause button' when those anger bubbles come so your anger doesn't overflow onto others?"

All of a sudden, his two brown eyes opened wide and a

light went on in his little heart. In fact, at the end of their family time, her son prayed that God would help him "push the pause button" when he got angry with his sister.

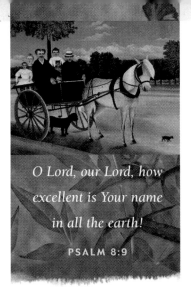

O Lord, our Lord, how excellent is Your name in all the earth!

PSALM 8:9

Using creativity instead of a lecture doesn't just help in addressing a problem area. It can also answer basic questions your child might have about his or her faith. For example, one Dad asked his sons the question, "How can God be real if we can't see Him?"

To help answer the question, he asked each child to blow up a balloon. They couldn't see the air going into the balloon, but when they counted to three and let their balloons go, they could see the reality of something "unseen" pushing their balloons through the air!

Yet another family decided to drive out to a city park after dark. Far away from the city lights, they walked to the middle of a soccer field and spread out a large blanket. Then, by flash-light, they read Psalm 8 a wonderful picture of God creating the heavens and earth. Looking up at a million stars while reading about the One who put them there was a lesson in faith none of them ever forgot.

God's Word is unchanging and timeless, but by using different methods to teach it, you can see eyes opened and hearts changed.

awn was a new Christian who struggled mightily with her past. She had come from an alcoholic home with an angry, hurtful father. Looking for love in all the wrong places, she became sexually involved in her early teens.

Until her late twenties, she found every new relationship like a desert mirage. Promising to quench her thirst for genuine love, immorality actually became choking sand. Then after college, she moved in with a Christian roommate, a young woman her age who told her about Someone who wouldn't leave, forsake, or abuse her. Someone who could change her life and free her from the cycle of sin she was in.

Like the woman at the well, who dipped in marriage seven times and found only sand, Dawn found the Living Water that Christ offered one beautiful day. She came to Christ and diligently sought to live a godly life. But there was *that one thing* that hindered her . . . she never felt really, truly forgiven.

Nearly every day, and sometimes several times a day, she would feel the cold edge of shame and guilt from her promiscuous past. A picture would come back, or the jagged edge of a memory. Then a clammy feeling of shame would set in, and she felt defeated and discouraged.

Three years after coming to Christ, Dawn fell in love and finally married a wonderful man in her church. Yet on the night of their honeymoon, she sat in tears in their hotel room.

She had not stayed pure before marriage, and she couldn't shake the pain and shame she felt after wearing the white dress and taking those vows of commitment. But a wise husband did something that changed her life and attitude instantly . . . a change that has stuck now for ten years.

On their wedding night, Dawn's husband knew of her feelings of guilt and shame. So he decided to do more than just dab her tears.

He decided to wash her feet.

As his new bride sat on the bed, he came out with a basin of warm water and a towel. And as Jesus had done with the obstinate Peter, he washed her feet as a symbol of what God had done for her soul.

> *No one is useless in this world who lightens the burden to anyone else.*
>
> **CHARLES DICKENS**

As he read her the Scriptures, Dawn was so moved that she broke into tears. In the humbling act of having her feet washed, she truly felt God's forgiveness for the first time in her Christian life. And since then, she has never doubted its reality.

Am I suggesting you have a "foot-washing" ceremony for your family?

Actually, it wouldn't be a bad idea for a powerful, life-changing lesson in forgiveness. But at least talk through the passage in which Peter's feet are washed (John 13) or through the subject of forgiveness with your family.

Ask whether anyone in your family needs to ask forgiveness . . . or needs to receive it.

What a comfort it is to a child's heart to know there's a place to wash away sin and shame.

Thanks to Jesus . . . who washes us clean.

People often reminisce about the Roaring Twenties as a time of glamour and gangsters. But for many, it was the front door to the 1930s and to the greatest depression we've ever faced as a country.

Four out of ten people were out of work in the '30s. Today, a 4 percent unemployment rate is typical.

Stock markets were in chaos. Today, they are skyrocketing.

The world was recovering from World War I and was facing the rumblings of a madman named Hitler who wanted to start another.

If ever a nation needed a message of hope and assurance, it was then. In fact, people longed for hope and direction. Perhaps that's why they listened so intently to one man's voice each Sunday afternoon, but not on television. For the most part, television was an experiment back then. Instead, they listened on the radio to what would be called Fireside Chats.

Each Sunday, Franklin Delano Roosevelt put forth a message that better times were ahead . . . prosperity was around the corner . . . and courage would keep us until then.

But then one day, he gave a very different message.

Roosevelt had gone to St. John's Episcopal Church on a January morning in 1938 to ask for divine guidance for the nation.

Reporters rushed up to him and asked . . . *or demanded,* *"Give us a word for the country . . . give us a word for the country!"*

And he did.

"I'll give you a word," FDR said.

"I request that the text of the Fifteenth Psalm be printed on the

front page of every paper in America. There could be no better word for our country" (New York Times, March 5, 1938, "Roosevelt Says 'Old Ship of State Is on Same Course'").

And, yes, hundreds of papers, large and small, carried the Fifteenth Psalm on the front page.

Could you just hear the critics today?

A *psalm* when we're in need of national healing? Publish a poem when so many people are out of work? Highlight an *ancient song* when economic times are tough and worldwide challenges are mounting?

Absolutely.

I wish it would happen today!

While Psalm 15 has about as much chance of appearing on the front page of today's papers as the news that prayer is allowed back in our schools, it remains the very message our country—and our families—need.

Psalm 15 is only five verses.

It shares two questions . . . and ten traits of a godly man or woman. And if lived out in our homes, it could change lives . . . and our nation.

Which brings me to this quiet thought.

How about getting out your Bible, looking up Psalm 15, and taking FDR's advice?

Read Psalm 15 at dinner tonight.

In troubled times or the best of times . . . there could be no better headline for your family.

Lord, who may abide in Your tabernacle?

Who may dwell in Your holy hill?

He who walks uprightly,

And works righteousness,

And speaks the truth in his heart;

He who does not backbite with his tongue,

Nor does evil to his neighbor,

Nor does he take up a reproach against his friend;

In whose eyes a vile person is despised,

But he honors those who fear the Lord;

He who swears to his own hurt and does not change;

He who does not put out his money at usury,

Nor does he take a bribe against the innocent.

He who does these things shall never be moved.

PSALM 15

One "chamber of commerce" December morning here in Phoenix, I was riding my mountain bike in a beautiful, rugged mountain preserve near my home.

Steep. Rocky. Challenging. Fun. Every trail is a combination of hard work going uphill and roller-coaster speed going down.

I had just rounded a corner when ahead of me I saw something I dreaded—*horses*. Slow, lumbering, trail horses that carried brightly colored tourists and clogged the narrow path we shared.

Forced to a crawl, I was frustrated being stuck behind those "overgrown snails." I couldn't wait for a wide area to pass. How dare they slow me down! With my full-suspension bike, I was on the fast track . . . so instead of waiting for a place to pass, I decided to take a scenic detour. In other words, "bomb" down the steep hill to our left to a wash below, then cut them off at the pass to get ahead of them.

Proud of my ingenuity, I shot past those four-legged roadblocks and down the hill—and into real trouble.

Right when I reached "warp speed" near the bottom of the hill, I suddenly saw a *huge rattlesnake* laying right in my path! (Insert your own image of a huge snake, but to me it looked like a T-rex!)

When God made rattlesnakes, He didn't give them tremendous hearing. (When was the last time you saw ears on a snake?) But He did give them a powerful sense of vibration and movement. As they lay on the ground, even at significant distances they can feel the vibrations of something slow and

lumbering, such as tourists on foot or on a horse. This allows them to scoot safely off of the trail and out of sight.

But put a forty-five year old on a mountain bike, reliving his youth and racing down a hill, and you can picture the frightening blur of vibrations and motion that I represented to that snake.

I will never forget the explosion of sight and sound as I fought to stop my bike without getting the snake wrapped in my spokes. No one had told this rattler that he couldn't make his trademark "Rrrrrrrrrrrr!" at the same time he struck. As I skidded to a crashing halt just inches short of the snake, he struck out repeatedly, trying to protect himself.

It was all over in a few, heart-stopping moments.

He finally decided to "make a run for it" (again defying conventional rattlesnake wisdom by rattling all the time he slid away), and I finally went back to breathing.

Having only a bike between you and a very large, very angry rattlesnake was a "striking" experience to say the least (pun intended). Yet in replaying the event, I learned a lesson that whispers to all parents . . . as well as to impatient bikers.

"Don't let the horses in front of you cause you to do something dumb."

If you need a translation, let me phrase it differently.

When Almighty God puts a "slow-moving" obstacle in front of your busy, hurried life . . . beware of cutting corners to try and get ahead.

You might just run into major trouble.

Unfortunately, I've seen many busy moms or dads on the

fast-track trail who suddenly turn the corner and catch sight of a time-consuming obstacle.

Not a four-legged one . . . but the two-legged variety.

Toddler or teenagers—their own sons or daughters.

For parents on the run—if they're honest—it can sometimes seem that kids are like a line of trail horses, slowing them down when they want to speed ahead with work or play or any one of a hundred other selfish things.

> *If we really have too much to do, there are some items on the agenda which God did not put there.*
> **ELISABETH ELLIOT**

Mom . . . Dad . . . don't let life in the fast lane lead you to look at your child as an obstacle instead of a gift. Don't shove them off to another baby-sitter on the weekends so you can do five more things that really could wait. Don't think that you can cut corners on spending time with them, or disciplining them, or training them to love God . . . and not run into a snake down the road.

It takes patience to ride behind trail horses until the path opens up. But that kind of patience and good common "horse" sense is available from Almighty God if we'll but ask.

65

I attended Dallas Seminary for my master's degree, where I majored in New Testament Greek. Now, lest you think I chose Greek because of some special aptitude for languages or extra measure of intelligence, let me set the record straight.

I stood in the wrong line!

On my first day at the seminary, I was told to declare a major. The shortest line had a sign above it that read *New Testament.* I was a new believer, and while *theology* or *homiletics* sounded fancier, I thought being a New Testament major sounded just great.

I didn't know until *after* I'd signed up that it meant New Testament *Greek!*

I certainly wasn't the best Greek student to go through Dallas Seminary. But four years and very little sleep later (and to the great surprise of several of my professors), I did graduate. Today, I still love to look at key words and phrases in Greek, particularly because so many Greek words have a picture behind them.

For example, *self-control* literally means "to pull in the reigns" of a horse. *Sin* means "missing the mark." The word for *forgiveness* means to "untie or loosen" the knots. And two words—*life and death*—have pictures behind them every parent should know.

In Greek, the word for *life* is *movement.*

Think about that picture for a moment.

Something that is alive . . . moves.

Move toward someone . . . connect with someone . . . like your children.

You add life to them and yourself when you move forward, stay engaged, stay active.

Can you guess the picture behind the word *death?*

It means "to stand alone."

For the Greek, dying was the ultimate isolation. As believers, dying means life—

Man was made to grow, not stop.

ROBERT BROWNING

"moving" all the way up to Heaven with our Lord! Death, on the other hand, meant to withdraw . . . to disconnect . . . to move away from others. Can you see the terrible application of this word?

When we isolate ourselves from our spouse or our children, the relationship will begin to die out.

In Proverbs we're told, "He who separates himself from his friend quarrels against all sound wisdom" (18:1, NASB).

Mom . . . Dad . . . there's a clear choice before you.

Choose life, and you're choosing to get and stay involved . . . and moving. Isolate yourselves from your church, spouse, family, or friends, and those relationships will dry up and die by degrees.

How about a family slogan that says, "As for me and my house . . . *we choose life*"?

Move in and toward the source of life itself, Jesus.

HEARING AIDS IN THE HOME

There's a story I once heard about an elderly grandfather who was very wealthy. The old man had been an artillery-man in World War II and had lost a good deal of his hearing from the blasting of cannons. His children knew his hearing had been steadily decreasing over the years. What they didn't know was that before their annual family reunion, he had breakthrough surgery to correct it.

While it might not seem like much, he regained almost 30 percent of his hearing after the surgery. In fact, along with his new hearing aids, his hearing was better than it had been in decades! Where once he had to look right at a person to be sure of what they said, now he could pick up conversations quite easily, even in the next room.

When he went in for a postoperative checkup, his doctor said to him, beaming with delight, "Your relatives must be very pleased to know that you can hear so much better."

"Oh, they don't know. I haven't told them yet," the old man said, chuckling. "I spent my time at the family reunion just listening . . . and I've changed my will twice!"

Dad and Mom, those little ears on the other side of the wall or down the hall don't need hearing aids in most cases. We may think they're busy or preoccupied, but children have a great sense of hearing our words . . . and our hearts. They have a keen ear to what's really going on in our marriage and an innate sense of the tension level in the home.

Several years ago, a couple came in for counseling precisely because of their son's "listening ear." The father had turned the stress of an insecure job into an excuse to raise his voice. His wife had a strong personality, and the two of them were like a thermometer. If one would raise the decibel level, then the other would match the tone. Talking could turn to shouting like the Arizona sun raising the mercury in August.

> *A word fitly spoken is like apples of gold in settings of silver.*
>
> **PROVERBS 25:11**

Both had come from a long line of dishonoring, loud marriages, and it seemed like "the sins of the fathers" would be passed down in their homes as well. That is, until the day their nine-year-old boy helped them "hear" what he and his sister were listening to every day.

Call it "entrapment" or "illegal wiretapping," but their son hid a pocket recorder in the kitchen, the place where his parents often argued.

Then the day came when he played a tape at dinner . . . and he finished by asking his parents to stop being "so mean to each other."

In Proverbs we read, "Pleasant words are like a honeycomb, sweetness to the soul and health to the bones" (16:24), and "He who has knowledge spares his words, and a man of understanding is of a calm spirit" (17:27).

But we also read, "An ungodly man digs up evil, and it is on his lips like a burning fire" (Prov. 16:27).

Your kids and mine already have "hearing aids" when it comes to our homes. May our words be restrained, sweet to listen to, and healing to their little lives and hearts.

69

My friend Gary Richmond is currently a single parent and pastor in California, but for ten years, he worked at the Los Angeles Zoo. He has also written one of my favorite books, *A View from the Zoo.* In it, he tells amazing stories of his time spent walking and talking to the animals. One story in particular has much to say to us as parents—it sends chills down my spine every time I hear it!

It happened the day Gary volunteered for a special assignment: there was a "problem" with one of the snakes. Not just *any* snake.

The main attraction in the snake exhibit was a thirteen-foot-long king cobra.

This type of cobra is so deadly that its bite has been known to kill an elephant who wandered too near! With this in mind, picture the zoo's king cobra, in molting season, trying to shed its skin . . . *only its old skin has snagged on the scar tissue around its left eye!*

The zoo needed helpers to go into the cage, capture the very angry snake, and help it shed its skin.

Four men entered the snake pit with the herpetologist. The curator of reptiles pinned the great snake's head while the reptile keepers held the snake firmly. Gary was responsible for giving surgical instruments to the doctor during the procedure.

Gary first helped the curator milk the snake of its venom by placing paper towels in its mouth. (If any of the helpers were bitten, then this *might* allow them to live long enough to get a shot of antivenin!)

The curator explained that he needed Gary to drain the

venom because his hands were sweaty and his fingers were cramping. He continued, "When I let him go, it may not be quick enough. More people are bitten trying to let go of snakes than when they grab them."

That's a thought worth repeating.

"More people are bitten trying to let go of snakes than when they grab them."

It's an easy application to our own lives.

Every day, people "pick up" something deadly, sinful, or potentially destructive, and later, these same people are bitten when trying to put it down.

For example, it was easy for Eve to reach up and pick the fruit. It was just as easy for Adam to take a bite and share in her sin. But how did they do at "putting it down" without being "bitten?"

In my counseling practice, I often see a husband or wife who has picked up a serpent.

Perhaps it is getting involved in an affair . . . and being "bitten" while trying to end it.

Perhaps it's lying . . . or cheating . . . or physical or emotional abuse.

Mom . . . Dad . . . it's important to teach our children this truth.

"Picking up" something sinful is ten times easier than putting it down—be it lying, stealing, slandering, or any other "secret sin" that one day *will* come to light.

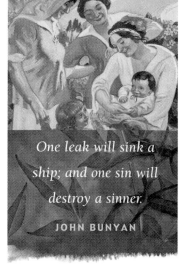

When King David fell into sin with Bathsheba, he tried to hide the immoral relationship he'd "picked up." The result: "When I kept silent [about my sin], my bones grew old through my groaning all the day long" (Ps. 32:3).

One leak will sink a ship; and one sin will destroy a sinner.

JOHN BUNYAN

His antivenin?

"I acknowledged my sin to You, and my iniquity I have not hidden. I said, 'I will confess my transgressions to the Lord,' and You forgave the iniquity of my sin" (v. 5).

73

MONUMENTS TO EMPTINESS

It was a great idea.

Build an architectural marvel in the middle of the Los Angeles Zoo that would become the "signature" gathering place. It's now called the Theme Building, and it overlooks a fair portion of the main zoo. As you near it, you'll see twin spires that ascend ten stories into the sky and a beautiful tiled roof. It is African, Indian, and Asian in appearance, and its motif sets the mood for the rest of the buildings throughout the zoo.

But there's a slight problem with this building.

The committee that worked with the architect could not agree on what should go *under* the twin spires and magnificent roof. So, when you arrive at the building, you see a million spires . . . standing over a dirt floor.

For Christian parents, there are a lot of lessons to glean here. Let me start with just one.

In the Gospel of John, our Lord speaks of how foolish it is to start a tower . . . and leave it unfinished (Luke 14:28). The incomplete project is a testimony to poor stewardship and a lack of wisdom. In that parable, our Lord is also speaking about more than just brick and mortar.

As parents, it's not enough to spend all our resources on the "outside." I'm all for nice homes and designer jeans (if you buy them on sale), but manicured lawns and great clothes won't make up for an unfinished inside. Our focus needs to be on our children's character and faith and on developing servants' hearts.

Don't settle for a beautiful exterior . . . with dirt floors in the interior.

Every second spent on the "inside" blesses your kids.

I do not ask for any crown
But that which all may win;
Nor try to conquer any world
Except the one within.

LOUISA MAY ALCOTT

NEIGHBORLY NEIGHBORS?

A pastor friend of mine sent me the story of a couple in his church who reached out to a new couple at church on Sunday. They sat next to these new people who had recently moved to their city. They exchanged pleasantries, and the new couple asked about their neighborhood.

"Oh, we live in a great neighborhood. The people are friendly, and it's a great place to live," they said. And then they listened sympathetically as the new couple shared just the opposite. They'd been in their house almost six months and still hadn't gotten to know their neighbors.

Imagine their embarrassment when the pastor's friends drove home from church that day . . . and their new friends from church pulled up in the driveway next door!

There is a word for reaching out to neighbors—the Bible calls it *hospitality,* and it's a mark of a growing Christian . . . and a Christian family.

In Romans, we're told that we're to be people "distributing to the needs of the saints, given to hospitality" (12:13).

In 1 Timothy, the description of a godly woman who could be placed on the widows role included one who was "well reported for good works . . . [and] has lodged strangers" (5:10).

The Book of Hebrews puts a celestial slant on what it means to be hospitable. "Do not forget to entertain strangers, for by so doing some have unwittingly entertained angels," we're told (13:2).

This brings me to a question and challenge: How's the hospitality level in your home?

Let's face it, in busy homes today, there's an almost-automatic assumption that "They're too busy to accept an invitation for lunch," or "I'm sure someone else has got them covered."

Those are good rationalizations, but poor theology. As parents, we're to model hospitality both inside and outside of our homes.

Every charitable act is a stepping-stone toward heaven.

HENRY WARD BEECHER

Robert E. Lee, the commanding general for the south in the Civil War, was a committed Christian who modeled hospitatlity. Several years after the war, Lee was traveling by train to Richmond. The general was deeply revered by the people of the south and was greeted with applause and honor when he boarded the train.

At one stop, an elderly woman entered the coach. Having no seat offered to her, she trudged down the aisle to the back of the car. Immediately, Lee stood up and gave her his place.

Several men then arose to give the general his seat.

"No, gentlemen," he said, "If there is none for this lady, there can be none for me!"

That's living out hospitality, not claiming celebrity status.

The odds are greatly against that elderly woman was an angel . . . but you never know.

Why not make it a family motto to treat others with heavenly hospitality? It's a clear mark of a caring home.

NEVER GIVE UP HOPE

Part of parenting, and everyday life, is maintaining hope and faith in difficult times. The importance of tenaciously holding onto hope is powerfully illustrated in Viktor Frankl's inspiring work, *Man's Search for Meaning*. Based on his experiences in a Nazi death camp, his core message is captured in a single tragic story.

Frankl, who was a medical doctor before he was imprisoned, writes,

"... My senior block warden, a fairly well-known composer and librettist, confided in me one day: 'I would like to tell you something, Doctor. I have had a strange dream. A voice told me that I could wish for something, that I should only say what I wanted to know, and all my questions would be answered. What do you think I asked? That I would like to know when the war would be over for me. You know what I mean, Doctor—for me! I wanted to know when we, when our camp, would be liberated and our sufferings come to an end.'

'And when did you have this dream?' I asked.

'In February, 1945,' he answered. It was then the beginning of March.

'What did your dream voice answer?'

Furtively he whispered to me, 'March thirtieth.'

When F—— told me about his dream, he was still full of hope and convinced that the voice of his dream would be right. But as the promised day drew nearer, the war news which reached our camp made it appear very unlikely that we would be free on the promised date.

On March twenty-ninth, F—— suddenly became ill and ran a high temperature. On March thirtieth, the day his prophecy had told

him that the war and suffering would be over for him, he became delirious and lost consciousness. On March thirty-first, he was dead. To all outward appearances, he had died of typhus."

Frankl's diagnosis?

"With his loss of belief in the future, he also lost his spiritual hold; he let himself decline and became subject to mental and physical decay."

> *The Christian's chief occupational hazards are depression and discouragement.*
>
> **JOHN STOTT**

For Frankl, seeing someone lose hope was a death sentence because it weakened his faith and ruined his physical health.

Steadfast hope versus loss of belief.

Spiritual growth versus sharp decline. Those are not just choices in a Nazi death camp; they're life and death realities.

Much of life comes down to those basic biblical choices as well. Even in the midst of trials, we need to take God at His Word: "Surely there is a future, and your hope will not be cut off" (Prov. 23:18, NASB). If you've faced a day—or a week—when the kids have been a handful . . . don't lose hope.

If you're facing financial stress, an unwanted move, or medical condition . . . don't lose hope. Take heart instead from the words of Paul. We're to stay "rejoicing in hope, patient in tribulation, continuing steadfastly in prayer" (Rom. 12:12).

79

magine you're sitting down to dinner in the cafeteria at Northwestern University. It's a bitter, cold night, and rain and wind whip off of Lake Michigan with a bone-chilling edge. Suddenly, a man bursts in and calls for volunteers. A ferry has run aground in the storm. People's lives are in great danger. They desperately need students to help in the rescue.

The year was 1896. Students rushed down to the water-front and formed themselves into rescue teams. Everyone who helped that terrible night was a hero. But there was one student who seemed to be everywhere. Time and again, he braved the near-freezing water to take a rescue rope to a struggling passenger. Before the night was over, he was credited with personally saving *seventeen people* from the sinking ship.

That student's name was Edward Spencer.

When all were safely ashore, he fell unconscious due to the cold and exhaustion. Other students carried him to his room, where his first words when revived were,

"Did I do my best? *Do you think I did my best?*"

Years later, the great evangelist R. A. Torrey was speaking in Los Angeles. In his sermon, he talked about this incident and even referred to Spencer's heroism.

"He's here!" shouted a man in the audience.

"Dr. Torrey," the man persisted, *"The Edward Spencer you speak of is here tonight!"*

And he was. More than fifty years had passed since that night. The audience cheered as Dr. Torrey invited him to the platform. Instead of a college student, it was an old man with sandy white hair that slowly climbed the steps.

Then he was asked what stood out most in his memory from that terrible, heroic night.

"Only this, sir," Spencer replied.

"Of the seventeen people I saved, *not one of them thanked me.*"

This brings to mind an incident in the Scriptures, doesn't it?

"Now it happened as He went to Jerusalem that He passed through the midst of Samaria and Galilee. Then as He entered a certain village, there met Him ten men who were lepers, who stood afar off. And they lifted up their voices and said, 'Jesus, Master, have mercy on us!' So when He saw them, He said to them, 'Go, show yourselves to the priests.' And so it was that as they went, they were cleansed" (Luke 17:11-14).

All came back to thank the Lord . . . right?

Wrong. Only one. And he was, of all things, a "despised Samaritan."

"So Jesus answered and said, 'Were there not ten cleansed?

Thou that has given so much to me, Give one thing more, a grateful heart. Not thankful when it pleaseth me, As if thy blessings had spare days; But such a heart, whose pulse may be Thy praise.

GEORGE HERBERT

But where are the nine? Were there not any found who returned to give glory to God except this foreigner?" (v. 17-18).

"And He said to him, 'Arise, go your way. Your faith has made you well'" (v. 19).

In Edward Spencer's case, the total was 0 for 17 in the thanks department.

For our Lord, it was slightly better—1 out of 10.

What's the score in your home?

Before you think about how thankful your children are, what score would you give *yourself* when it comes to giving thanks?

Do you regularly say *thank you* to the checker at the grocery store or the teller at the bank? Do your children see you thanking the pastor after a sermon, or do they see you taking his sermon apart? Do they see you thank their teacher at school, or their Sunday school teacher when you pick them up after church?

Cultivate thankfulness. Gratefulness is a learned skill . . . and if your children are to be thankful people, they'll learn it in large measure from you.

Teach your children to be that 1 out of 10—someone who says *thank you*.

People and the Lord will remember if they do it . . . or if they don't.

Recently, a friend e-mailed me the results of an assignment given to a group of six year olds. They were asked by their teacher, "What is a very important truth you've learned this year?"

As you can imagine, the responses were priceless.

➤ "Never, ever let your three-year-old brother hold a tomato for you."

➤ "Throw a ball at someone, they'll probably throw it back . . . harder."

➤ "Never turn on the DustBuster when you're holding your cat."

And then this priceless one that many six-year-old girls can relate to:

➤ "When your mom is mad at your dad, *never* let her brush your hair."

Behind these last endearing words is an important insight. Namely, anger at its worst runs downhill. Let's face it. It's easy to pass our frustration down to our loved ones . . . and not just when we brush their hair.

Take Jim for example. One of the city's "finest," he'd been a police officer for six years. After his shift in a particularly difficult part of the city ended, his frustration level was near zero when he came home to an active three year old. The first time his son saw him each day, he was angry and withdrawn.

Distance was quickly becoming the position of choice in that family . . . until Jim made a life-changing decision.

Jim had been meeting with a small group of men at his

church when one ex-soldier challenged Jim to do something that had helped him as a father in the service.

"Don't go home," he said, "until you've stopped the car for however long it takes to do a 'palms down-palms up.'"

Here's what he meant.

Every day, before Jim got home, he'd stop at a small baseball field and park his car. Then he'd take his palms and put them down on his legs. With "palms down," he'd mentally go through the day, praying over and confessing those hurtful, anger-producing, frustrating events he'd experienced. It was "out with the bad air" before inhaling the good.

After he'd prayed about the day's events and confessed his own sin, it was time for "palms up." That's when he would spend a few minutes praising God and asking the Lord to open up his life to Him and to his family.

Then Jim would drive into the driveway—and his family saw the difference immediately.

His son went from standing back from him to running to his car.

His wife went from worrying to praising—and falling even more in love with him.

> *Contentment is one of the flowers of heaven, and if we would have it, it must be cultivated . . . it is the new nature alone that can produce it.*
>
> **CHARLES SPURGEON**

85

Mom . . . Dad . . .
don't wait until your
relationship with your
spouse or children needs
artificial respiration. If
you're facing lots of
frustration during your
day—and are tempted to
let anger run downhill—
be proactive in that
simple exercise.

Palms down . . .
palms up. Out with the
bad . . . in with God's
best.

*"Then Aaron shall cast lots for the two goats:
one lot for the Lord and the other lot for the scapegoat.
And Aaron shall bring the goat on which the Lord's lot fell,
and offer it as a sin offering. But the goat on which the
lot fell to be the scapegoat shall be presented alive
before the Lord, to make atonement upon it, and
to let it go as the scapegoat into the wilderness."*

LEVITICUS 16:8–10

IN SEARCH OF A FAMILY SCAPEGOAT

F or the Old Testament Jews, a special ceremony took place every year on the Day of Atonement. Unfortunately, this ceremony still reflects what is happening in homes today.

The ceremony worked like this: two goats were chosen by lots, one to be sacrificed, the other to become a scapegoat. What was the purpose of the scapegoat?

Aaron, the high priest, would gather all the people together and lay his hands on the goat's head. In doing so, he symbolically transferred the sins of the nation onto that animal. The goat was then driven outside of the camp and forced into the wilderness to die.

In its proper biblical setting, the "scapegoat" was a picture of Christ's love and sacrifice. Jesus, the Lamb of God, was led outside of the city to be crucified. The Father laid our sins upon Him, and He became our "scapegoat" and our lamb of sacrifice (Rom. 3:25; Heb. 10:10).

While there is a redeeming nature to the Old Testament scapegoat and Christ's sacrifice, those lofty positives aren't true for a *family* scapegoat.

Family scapegoats grow up feeling like they're the cause of all their family's problems . . . and they're often told this. They're the loud one in a quiet home. Or the quiet one in a loud home. They're the musician who never made it as an athlete . . . or the child who is singled out as unwanted or a burden.

If we really want peace in the world, let us first love one another in the family.

MOTHER TERESA

Scapegoat children often bear burdens beyond their age or ability to understand. Like trying to plug into a faulty electrical outlet, their attempts to plug into their family for nurturing only lead to greater and greater "shocks."

God has already provided the ultimate sacrifice for our sins. He needs no other. And neither does He honor the "sacrifice" of one person in an unhealthy home who has been singled out to carry family problems or shame.

For all of us who grew up as "scapegoats," it's wonderful to know our Heavenly Father loves and accepts us just the way we are. And for all of us who are parents . . . may He help us to *not* pick out a scapegoat . . . but to see each child as a unique creation of Almighty God.

I admit it.

By nature, I'm a *lecturer* . . . not a listener.

Forget active listening or asking lots of clarifying questions.

My first reaction when one of the kids starts to share a problem or concern is to jump in and try to solve things— even if I really haven't heard what those "things" are from their perspective.

According to God's Word, there's a description for someone who "speaks before he hears" like that. It's called being a "shameless fool."

Proverbs 18:13 says, "He who answers a matter before he hears it, it is folly and shame to him."

Now, don't take offense and throw this book across the room. That's God's assessment, not mine.

After all, I'm too often in the "fool" camp myself, convicted by how little I really listen to my loved one.

Listening . . . not lecturing. That's the key.

Thankfully, I had a wonderful teacher who showed me how listening can powerfully bless a child of any age.

During my high school years, my twin brother Jeff and I used to come in from our dates and flop down on either side of my mom, who was already in bed. It was late at night, long after she had gone to sleep. But that's when we wanted to talk.

I'm not sure how we got into that ritual. But with sports and school activities, it seemed the only time we had to talk was late on a weekend night. That's when we'd share not only about our evening, but also about our dreams and hopes, our heartaches, and the trials we faced.

Being naturally sensitive, it quickly dawned on me that perhaps Mom didn't *want* to be woken up. After all, she'd worked all week and often had to go to work the next day.

I'll never forget the first time I asked her about it.

Well-timed silence has more eloquence than speech.

M. T. TUPPER

"Mom," I said, as two teenage football players snuggled on either side of her like five year olds, "Does it bother you that we wake you up to talk like this? . . . I know you have to go to work tomorrow."

It was pitch dark in the room when the best mom in the world answered.

"Honey," she said. "You wake me up anytime . . . I can always go back to sleep, but I won't always have you boys around to talk to."

I don't know when I've ever felt so loved.

So cared for . . . so special to someone.

All because she carved out time to *listen,* even when it was late.

Mom . . . Dad . . . I know it takes time and effort to listen . . . *especially* when it's early or late. But it's a "quiet" way to bless your children and leave them with a memory of your love.

*Making the decision
to have a child is
momentous—it is
to decide forever
to have your heart
go walking outside
your body.*

ELIZABETH STONE

Several years ago, in the home of some close friends of ours, the mom, dad, and all five children were gathered around the dinner table. As often happens in this very verbal family, everyone was talking at the same time—except their youngest child.

After their five year old repeatedly tried to squeeze into the conversation, he finally stood up on his chair and screamed at the top of his voice!

His blood-curdling cry stopped the chattering cold.

With all eyes riveted on his little face, he said,

"What's the matter around here? *Doesn't anyone have any ears?*"

Mom . . . Dad . . . as funny as that may seem, let me ask you a tough question.

Does your family have "ears" for each other?

Many of us are masters at passive listening. It's easy to give our kids a sideways glance or condescending smile when we're still watching the game or movie. God's Word describes a way to make sure your kids know that your family has "ears!"

Learn to listen with your eyes.

The eye is the window of the soul.

H. POWERS

It might surprise you to learn that listening is more a function of using your eyes than your ears. Communication experts tell us that verbal words comprise only about 7 percent of what we communicate. Though tone of voice is 38 percent, body language is 55 percent. So a huge portion of listening is done with your eyes.

Solomon, the wisest man who ever lived, dropped an incredibly helpful communication hint for those who want close relationships.

"The light of the eyes rejoices the heart," he wrote (Prov. 15:30).

Most of us have had the experience of walking into a room and seeing somebody's eyes "light up" when he or she sees us.

That momentary sparkle in another person's eyes communicates volumes. It's like someone flipping on an internal light switch. It's a look that carries the message, *"I hear what you're saying. You're important to me. I care for you. I'm excited to be with you."*

What message do your children see in your eyes? Do your eyes "light up" when they come to you and want to talk or sit around the table?

Having "bright eyes" is a quiet, powerful way to bless your children . . . and your spouse. Try it today.

PURE-WATER PARENTING

Imagine going on a hike with your family. The children are young and thrilled to be outside in the Great Outdoors. They're determined to hike all the way across the forest . . . which means gamely hiking for at least two hundred yards before they call a halt and cry out, *"Daddy . . . Mommy . . . We need a drink of water, please!"*

"Sure, kids," you say.

Then you fill a cup to the rim for each of them . . . with muddy, filthy water.

Would you give a child you love a drink of muddy water?

Of course not. It's unthinkable.

Which brings me to this quiet thought.

How pure is the water you're handing to your child?

I'm not talking about what comes out of a canteen. But what comes out of your mouth.

The Book of James compares our words to pure or muddy water. We're told that with our mouth "we bless our God and Father, and with it we curse men, who have been made in the similitude of God. Out of the same mouth proceed blessing and cursing" (James 3:9-10).

Fresh water and dirty . . . from the same canteen we carry inside us?

The apostle's conclusion, *"My brethren, these things ought not to be so"* (v. 10).

If we're honest, pure-water words can be a challenge for some of us parents. For example, I heard the story of a young boy who was driven to preschool one day by his father. The next day, his mother took him to school. As she was getting

Create in me a clean heart, O God, and renew a steadfast spirit within me.

PSALM 51:10

the youngster out of his car seat, he looked up at his mother and asked, "Mom, where are all the idiots?"

"Excuse me?" asked the mom.

"Where are all the idiots this morning?" he asked again emphatically. "Daddy drove us to school yesterday, and we saw six idiots!"

It's a challenge to tame the tongue when we're driving, or watching biased political coverage, or when we're tired and grumpy.

But little kids are drinking in our words.

Do they hear gossip, swearing, criticism, or lying?

Or words of blessing and encouragement?

How pure are the words you're holding out to your child?

QUIET WHISPERS FROM GOD'S HEART FOR PARENTS

All of us long to know that we're special and needed, that we fit in. That we came onboard wanted, rather than by accident—a welcome addition, rather than a family disruption. We need to hear words of acceptance often, and from a parent if possible. Even more, we need to hear Almighty God Himself say, "I choose you." To know that He specifically designed our button nose or curly hair (Pss. 119:73 and 139!) and that we're His beloved and He our Father.

Children who grow up with a strong sense of belonging to their parents and the Lord gain ground on those who do not. Yet as important this is, there are many children who will never experience that level of love.

Does that mean they're just damaged goods?

Not if you look at Judy.

She certainly could have grown up feeling worthless and like a failure.

Judy grew up in a home where her parents showed her little love and conditional acceptance. She was an accident, a burden, the youngest of six children, and six years behind the others.

Her siblings picked up the negative chorus constantly teasing her. If it wasn't her "scraggly" hair or her "turned-up" nose, they loved to tell neighborhood children, "Judy really isn't our sister . . . We found her when she was a baby abandoned in a vacant lot—and we'd like to send her back!"

Talk about a prescription for insecurity! But how does Judy feel as a wife and parent of young children today?

Very special and valuable.

In fact, today Judy has one of the best marriages, and is one of the best moms I know.

But how?

In Judy's case, and thousands like her, she ran into "special agents." "Spies" crept in and stole hurtful words and replaced them with God's love.

Who are these "secret agents" of blessing? Grandparents.

Her grandparents lived just a few houses down as Judy was growing up. Her grandfather was a retired carpenter with bright, blue eyes and strong, gentle arms that hugged her every day. And her grandmother had the best lap to sit on for miles around.

Every day after school, she would run to her grandparents' home for a cookie or snack before heading home to the ridicule . . . and she wasn't just looking for something for her stomach. She was filling up her heart and soul before she headed into "the desert."

A little flour and sugar might make a good cookie, but even better were the words and actions that came warm and fresh from her grandparents. To them, she was always special, deeply loved, and greatly valuable. They, not her parents, took Judy to church and gave her a promise ring. They held out hope for a positive future for her. She devoured their "cookies for the heart" and now gives them freely to her own children and others.

It wasn't an obvious show . . . after all, they were "secret agents." But when her parents were too busy to listen, Gramma and Grandpa had nothing but time.

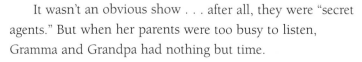

When there was a problem with another girl at school, she received counsel and prayers, not an impatient lecture.

When Judy was feeling hurt or discouraged, Gramma would cradle Judy's head in her lap and gently stroke her hair. She'd listen as long as Judy wanted to talk, speaking only loving, comforting words and saying "Mmmmmm," "My, my," and "Bless your poor little heart. You're really hurting aren't you?"

There are only two lasting bequests we can hope to give our children. One of these is roots, the other wings.

HOLDING CARTER

Just feeling like she was being heard, even without being given a solution, gave Judy the freedom to unload the hurt and soak in healing love.

Mom . . . Dad . . . here's a quiet thought for today.

Even if you're years away from getting your AARP card . . . or weren't blessed with grandparents like Judy's . . . be a "grandparent" to your child today.

Available.

Accepting.

Loving.

Encouraging.

God's "special agent" when it comes to giving out unconditional love.

THE TALE OF TWO POTS

There is a folk tale told about two clay pots.
It's a story that whispers something important that you—
and your child—need to know.

It seems there were once two pots.

Each was carried by the king's water bearer on the end of a long pole.

One pot was perfect. Well decorated. Without the slightest imperfection.

The other pot was very pretty too, made of the same good clay and bright colors . . . except it had a single crack.

Each day, the king's water bearer would make the trek from the palace to the river below and would fill up each pot. That's where the problem began.

While both started out full of water, the cracked pot left a trail of droplets along the path.

As the days and years passed, the cracked pot came to dread the day's journey. It was always the same, watching the perfect pot pour out his contents into the king's cistern . . . without having lost a single drop. Then the cracked pot would pour out his offering, which seemed so much less.

Which was why, at last, the cracked pot spoke up.

"Oh, water bearer," said the pot, "please replace me. I have tried my hardest, but I know I've failed to be what you want me to be."

"That is not so," said the water bearer.

"It is!" said the cracked pot. "Just look at my offering next to the perfect pot's. It's so little. I'm ashamed of what I bring before the king."

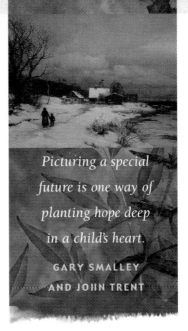

Picturing a special future is one way of planting hope deep in a child's heart.

GARY SMALLEY
AND JOHN TRENT

"Enough!" said the water bearer, his face as dark as a storm cloud. "The perfect pot fulfills its purpose, that is true. But it was the king himself who picked you . . . not me. And you have fulfilled his plan."

"I have?" said the cracked pot, full of confusion.

"Have you not noticed the hill we walk up every day? Look now," he said pointing, and all along one side of the path grew beautiful flowers. "Have you not seen me spreading seeds as I walked up the hill?"

And then he said in a kinder voice, "Those flowers grow from your loss, little pot . . . and they please the king."

And at last the cracked pot saw that—crack and all—he did fulfill his master's purpose.

"But now, O Lord, You are our Father; we are the clay, and You our potter; and all we are the work of Your hand" (Isa. 64:8).

TOSSING IN THE TOWEL

The year was 1952. For my mother, it was a time of heartache, pain, and transition. It had been less than six months since my father had walked out for good, which left her alone to raise and be the sole supporter for a two year old and three-month-old twins. That's three children under the age of three, and she had no school background, no displaced-homemaker programs, no child support, no alimony, and no family money to lessen the blow.

It's tough being a single parent today, and it was just as challenging in the 1950s. Without a college degree or ever having entered the workforce, Mom was forced to balance raising three preschool boys and working a full-time clerical job. Added to these was her ticket to a better job—night school.

I'm proud to say that besides being a great mom, my mother did graduate from business school. She went on to have a wonderful career in the savings and loan business. In fact, she became so accomplished that, in 1959, she got an article and a black-and-white ink portrait on the front page of the *Wall Street Journal!*

But by her own account, none of that would have happened if it hadn't been for one act of kindness from a classmate whose name she can't even remember.

During those early days of business school, Mom had a horrible time with typing and, especially, with her typing teacher. Recently retired from the army, he bullied his students like a drill sergeant with a sore tooth. In particular, he seemed to delight in tormenting my mom.

He relished in pulling out wadded pieces of paper from

her trash can. He'd thunder at her that she'd never be a good typist and should spare him the aggravation and just quit the class. (Remember this is 1952, when such actions were called motivation, not workplace harassment!)

With all the pressures of work and home, and knowing that typing was a required part of her curriculum, she became more error prone because of his scare tactics. Finally, after a particularly cutting outburst, Mom walked out of class with her head down and tears in her eyes. Maybe she should quit, she thought. But a schoolmate stepped in and changed the course of her life.

"Honey," came a soft, southern voice from a round, pretty face. "You just hang there, ya' hear. That old boy's just putting on airs."

"Now, starting tomorrow, you fold those papers you're throwing away in the trash. That way they don't stack up so much. He'll think you're doing better and stop picking on you."

And then she took my mom's arm and said, kindly, but with conviction, "And don't quit, Zoa. You're going to make it—I know you will."

> To have a good friend
> is the purest of all
> God's gifts, for it is
> a love that has
> no exchange
> of payment.
>
> **FRANCES FARMER**

With that, she was gone.

That night, while she was at the end of her rope, a few seconds of compassion, a single suggestion, and a few words of hope gave Mom the courage to come back one more day. My mom had renewed hope. (And now she carefully folded each paper she threw away!) Then her teacher made his daily stop at her desk. But this time, instead of blasting her, he gave her his first backhanded compliment.

"I guess Zoa is finally getting with things," he said grudgingly after inspecting her wastebasket. And then he walked away to torment some other "paper wadder."

Sometimes, it's the smallest of things that can change a friend's life. The Bible puts it this way, "Do not withhold good from those to whom it is due, when it is in the power of your hand to do so" (Prov. 3:28).

Dad . . . Mom . . . be that kind of friend to your friends and neighbors. But even more, be that kind of friend to your child.

Teach them by your actions to bless their classmates or the other players on their team. You'll be teaching them a skill that might not put their friend on the front page of the paper . . . but it can put Christ's love in their heart.

THE WORST OF WAKE-UP CALLS

ou could have heard a pin drop in the room. Nearly one hundred men, almost all of them fathers, had lumps in their throats, and many had tears in their eyes.

That's saying something for average guys who usually get choked up about as often as Halley's comet appears.

But it happened one day at a men's Bible study I taught.

I'd been teaching a series on "wake-up calls" in the Bible.

There was the one Jonah received when he was tossed into the belly of a whale. And Peter's wake-up call was provided by a rooster who crowed three times. And of course, Saul's blinding wake-up call on the road to Damascus that changed his life—and his name to Paul.

But that morning, I started our time by having a friend named Keith share a personal wake-up call he'd received.

Twenty-five years ago, Keith had two babies. Both demanded his time and attention. One was a beautiful, energetic son named Brian. The other was a brand new "baby" business he was starting out of his garage.

Keith shared that while Brian had a rare set of lungs, his new business cried louder. So one night, Keith made his choice.

"I remember the night, men," he said. "I felt pulled apart by work and home, so I just decided to let my wife deal with Brian. I'd go grow my business."

And he did.

From a garage to an office warehouse, to warehouses in eleven states, Keith built a state-of-the-art company. Keep in mind that Keith loved his children. In fact, in addition to Brian, they soon had four children . . . but by then he had nearly four hundred employees.

Keith shared that he always . . . always . . . comforted himself with this thought: "I'm doing this for Brian and the other kids. All these hours on the job are making it possible for us to kick back one day and spend quality time together."

And that day finally came when he sold his business.

There is a powerful, almighty God who is even more concerned about our children than we are. He is our partner in parenting.

SUSAN ALEXANDER YATES

It was more money than he and his wife ever dreamed of having when they started their company. And now, at last, he'd have time to spend with his kids.

As a "first" for their family, he notified his wife that they were all going to Hawaii! They could afford the best now, and it would be that "vacation that got away" when the kids and business were young.

He followed through and got the tickets . . . and the hotel reservations . . . and the travel folders.

What Keith didn't factor in was the police.

They showed up on January 3, 1993.

His wake-up call came at 4:45 a.m.

It began with a loud pounding, rousting him out of bed, sending him stumbling down the dark hallway to the front doorstep.

Was this the Wilson residence?

Yes.

Was he Keith Wilson?

Yes, he was.

Did he have a son named Brian?

Yes . . ., he stammered. He did.

"We're very, very sorry, but Brian has been in a bad accident," they said.

How bad?

"He's dead."

They came and left in less than two minutes. In a daze, Keith had to walk down the hall and tell his wife their twenty-year-old son was dead.

"Men," Keith told us with faltering speech and tearful eyes.

"Don't wait . . . Don't wait to tell your children you love them. Don't wait to spend time with them. A hundred times I've prayed to God and asked Him to give me just one more minute with Brian. To hold him. To tell him I was proud of him. To tell him I loved him. Just one minute . . ."

We all got a wake-up call that morning . . . and a tear-stained lesson about why we as parents shouldn't "wait" to love our children.

NEEDED FOR PARENTS AND CHILDREN: A ZIPPER FOR YOUR HEART

et a seventy-four-year-old man and a four-year-old boy side-by-side and they might not look like they have much in common. But one grandpa and his grandson did—especially one hot summer's day when they peeled off their T-shirts to go swimming.

With their shirts off, you could that see each wore a long, dramatic scar running the length of his chest.

Danny, the four year old, actually got his scar first. It came from major corrective heart surgery following his first birthday. His grandfather got his scar the previous year, after emergency bypass surgery.

Danny's grandfather told me something precious his grandson said as they "compared scars" that summer day.

"Grandpa," Danny said, *"Do you think the doctors gave us a zipper so that Jesus could get into our hearts easier?"*

Leave it to a child to turn a traumatic event into a picture of faith.

Forget the theology of "heart zippers" for a moment.

Linger over what Danny said.

"Do you think the doctors gave us a zipper so that Jesus could get into our hearts easier?"

Let me put it another way.

Does that "zipper" God gave you . . . *that scar you carry* . . . make your heart more open to the things of God?

I meet parents almost every day who carry "scars" of various sorts.

Broken homes growing up.

Marriage partners who bailed out.

Businesses that failed . . . a trusted partner who failed them. Prodigals who have broken their hearts.

Cuts to our self-worth . . . slashes to our best, brightest dreams . . . wounds that we still carry and that can make us afraid to "bear all" and open up to anyone . . . lest they see the scar.

I think Danny has the right idea.

He chose to look at his scar in a positive way. As a mark of openness to God . . . not as a sign of failure or shame.

Mom . . . Dad . . . do you carry a scar today?

So does the Lover of your soul.

"The other disciples therefore said to him, 'We have seen the Lord.' So he said to them, 'Unless I see in His hands the print of the nails, and put my finger into the print of the nails, and put my hand into His side, I will not believe" (John 20:25).

And Thomas did see His scars.

"And after eight days . . . He said to Thomas, 'Reach your finger here, and look at My hands; and reach your hand here, and put it into My side. Do not be unbelieving, but believing'" (v. 26-27).

Our Lord Jesus, even in all His glory in heaven today, still bears those scars. The apostle John saw Him standing in all His resurrected glory, "a Lamb as though it had been slain" (Rev. 5:6).

You have a mighty God. Strong enough to turn your scars into "zippers" that open your heart to His love and strengthen your faith.

Just like Thomas . . . and a little four-year-old boy.

"Thomas answered and said to Him, 'My Lord and my God!'" (John 20:28).

*Those who keep secrets
from God keep their
distance from God.
Those who are honest
with God draw
near to God.*

MAX LUCADO

ecently, my family and I had the privilege of going on a cruise to Alaska. It was a trip filled with breathtaking views . . . and one heartbreaking incident.

Cindy and the girls had finished breakfast and headed back to our cabin. As I sat finishing my coffee, watching the incredible scenery slide by outside the window, a very despondent young man and his mother came and sat down near me.

"But why Mom?" the nine or ten year old blurted out, oblivious to those around him. "Why did he even bother to come?"

You could see his mother struggle to frame her answer.

"Well," she said. "At least he's here. And he did pay for all of us to come on this trip."

"He's not here," her son shot back. "He's been on the phone or on his computer the whole time." And then came the shot to the heart. "He doesn't even look at me."

Something powerful happens when we look, really look at another person. The Book of Proverbs puts it this way, "Bright eyes make the heart glad" (15:30).

When someone looks at us with eyes that are lit up with warmth and love, it touches us deeply. When someone, like that father on the cruise, looks past us but never at us, it can scar us deeply.

Mom . . . Dad, we can learn a lesson from Someone who took the time to really look at others. If you have a Bible near, open it to the Book of Luke. Jesus "looked at" the rich young ruler (18:24, NASB), He "looked up" at Zaccheus (19:5), and He "looked at" the disciples as He told them He would be rejected and would suffer and die (20:17). He also "looked up"

and saw the poor widow who gave her mite as a sacred offering (21:1), and He "looked at" Peter after he had denied Him three times (22:61).

Jesus looked at people when He was with them. Really looked at them.

Even when he was tired, or troubled, or busy, or happy, or sad.

Small is the number of people who see with their eyes and think with their minds.

ALBERT EINSTEIN

This week, I'd encourage you to try a homework assignment. Really look at your spouse when you walk in from work. Perhaps even take her hand or nod in understanding as you talk to her. And with your children, really look at them. Not past them to the next interesting thing on television. Look at *them*.

While I was teaching a group of people recently, I asked them to pick one person they really appreciated and share what character trait they liked best about them. One lady immediately volunteered. She picked her husband.

"What trait do you most appreciate about him?" I asked.

"He's like a camera," she said. "With a zoom lens. When he talks to me, I feel like he drops everything and really focuses on me. He does the same thing with each of the kids."

You focus on a person by looking at them, really looking at them. May that be a trait that your children always remember about you.

assie Bernall was like all of the other students at her high school that April morning. She was counting down the days until the end of school, counting on a little extra time in the library to give her a better grade on a test. She was also counting on a life spent in reflecting her new love for Jesus, especially after turning away from drugs and having dabbled in witchcraft.

Her parents too were counting on her coming home from school that day, just like every other day before that one. But April 20, 1999, wasn't like other days. For no one counted on the two students who had turned into killers, blasting their way through the school and finally ending up in the library.

That terrible morning in Littleton, Colorado, students were killed in hallways and classrooms. They were gunned down for being athletes, or black, or for no reason at all. But Cassie was murdered for her faith.

Perhaps knowing about her changed life or seeing the cross she wore around her neck, one of her classmates/killers leveled a shotgun at Cassie. He then asked her if she believed in God. Without hesitation, she replied, "Yes, I believe in God."

In less time than it took for Cassie to utter those words of faith, she was killed. Her death, along with the deaths of a heroic teacher and too many of her classmates, made national headlines. But her confession of faith has made a huge difference in the lives of thousands of people of faith.

"Yes, I believe" has become a rallying cry for Christian youth across our country. At National Day of Prayer events on May 6, 1999, thousands of high school students took part in rallies honoring our Lord. At one such event, Jennifer Kuzia, an eighteen-year-old senior, summed up her thoughts on Cassie's last act of faith.

"That's true faith," she was quoted as saying in *USA Today,* "I'd like to believe I'd be like that."

We'd all like to be like that.

To have Cassie's courage and faith. To have that kind of commitment, even when everything is at stake.

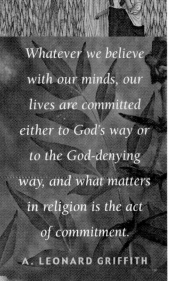

Whatever we believe with our minds, our lives are committed either to God's way or to the God-denying way, and what matters in religion is the act of commitment.

A. LEONARD GRIFFITH

There is no way to prepare ourselves or our children for such a moment in time like Cassie faced. However, we can help our children see, by our example, an unswerving commitment to them, to our spouse, and, most importantly, to Christ.

God's Word gives us a challenging description of ten characteristics of a godly person. The Fifteenth Psalm of David tells us that a godly person "swears to his own hurt and does not change" (4).

"Swears to his own hurt"—What does that mean, and how is it a picture of commitment?

When someone made a commitment in the Hebrew

language, they used an oath to seal the fact. We still do that in courtrooms today when a witness swears to tell the "whole truth and nothing but the truth." In short, swearing before a judge constitutes a solemn commitment to be honest. (Certain political figures excepted!)

Psalm 15 gives us a "picture" of what real commitment looks like. In Hebrew, the language of the Old Testament, "swearing" to something literally meant to "seven yourself."

Do you get "the picture"? If not, try an experiment. Cut a single, twelve-inch strand of kite string and see if you can pull on it with both hands until it snaps. Most people can snap a single strand with a minimal amount of effort. But then wrap seven strands of kite string together and see if you can break them. If your name isn't Arnold Swartzamuscle, then breaking a seven-strand cord is nearly impossible.

That's the literal picture behind swearing to something. When we make a commitment, we're "sevening" ourselves by making our commitments as strong as a seven-strand rope.

That type of hard-to-break commitment is what Cassie showed her killers . . . and the world.

Lord, may our faith be "seven strands strong" as we love, bless, and encourage our children. Amen.